DANIEL'S BOOK OF PRAYERS

Written by
Nadine Miller-Campbell
and
Daniel Campbell

Illustrated by
Dehstin Campbell

Copyright © 2020

All rights reserved. This book is protected by the copyright laws of the United States of America. No part of this book may be used or reproduced by any means, graphic, electronic, or mechanical, including photocopying, recording, taping, or by any informational storage retrieval system without the written permission of the author, except in case of brief quotations embodied in critical articles and reviews. For permission, write to author at the email address and webpage below:

nadinemillercampbell@yahoo.com

ISBN: 978-1-7321710-3-9(paperback)
978-1-7321710-2-2(ebook)

DEDICATION

To my great-grandfather, Vincent White and Great-grandmother Eulalee White, thank you for transferring the art of story-telling to my nanny Joyice White.

Joyice White (nanny), Glassford Miller (Roy, grandfather), Michael Campbell (grandfather), and Maxine Kelly (Grandmother), thank you for all your prayers.

To Latoya Reid-Turner, Kerry-ann Ellington-Robinson, Dehstin Campbell, and my dad Conrad Campbell, thank you for your help in marking this book a success. To Debbie Miller-Curtis, Pastor Keith, and my mom Nadine Miller-Campbell, your faith inspired me.

LETTER TO PARENTS

Daniel's Book of Prayer is written, specifically to encourage and facilitate conversations between adults and children about prayer. It is a great way to introduce children to pray during devotions at home or church.

Daniel has expressed himself powerfully throughout this book to motivate children across the world, not only to believe in prayer but to pray every day.

As parents, it is our responsibility to start prayer as early as possible in our children.

This book will inspire them to learn simple but effective ways of how to communicate with God. As they grow older, they will become familiar with prayer, and as a result, later develop the habit of praying.

Daniel truly believes in his heart that prayer gives him a connection to heaven and his Heavenly Father, who gives him access to the supernatural powers of healing and change in the spiritual realm by faith.

Children are innocent and they capture the heart of God. According to Matthew 19:14 (KJV) "But Jesus, said suffer little children, and forbid them not, to come unto me: for of such is the kingdom of heaven."

As parents, we should be encouraged that there is hope for our future because of our praying children.

I am **DANIEL**,
and I am seven years old.
I love to pray,
and prayer gives me power.
It gives me access
to supernatural help.
When I am older,
I would love to be a pastor,
and prayer will help me
to be a great pastor!

I love God. I talk to him a lot. He talks to me too, and prayer is one of the ways we communicate.
I can use this superpower anytime and anywhere.
I can pray in my mind, in a whisper, with an inside voice, or I can shout it out loud.

There are many different forms of prayers,
and many different prayer positions
mentioned in the Bible.
Do you have a favorite position?
I love to lie down with my feet up. Sometimes at church,
we pray with our hands lifted or kneeling.

You can pray in your favorite position,
or you can use one of these positions:

Prayer is universal, simple, and effective. It doesn't require a lot, just faith. If you want to see the power of prayer, you must believe that God can do what you are asking.

You can pray for anyone, anything, anytime, or anywhere. There are no restrictions on where you pray, what time you pray, or how often you pray.

I love to pray because it gives me power!

Prayers are used in many different ways.

You can use prayer as a tool, or a secret weapon to help you fight the enemy, and escape his evil traps. He is the villain behind the evil we see, for example, lying and stealing. Most superheroes have a supernatural power that helps them fight against the enemy. Prayer is my superpower!

I use prayers to call for help. God has given us this powerful tool to communicate with him any time of day. Prayer is like a cellular phone that you can use to dial 911 or whatever number you use to call for help.

We can use prayer as a signal to call God. Whenever you are in trouble, or you don't know what to do, start praying, and heaven will rescue you.

You can pray for anyone in the world that needs God's help.
You should always pray for yourself.
Look for ways how you can use this powerful tool.
Sometimes my mom and dad need some extra help,
and they pray and ask God for his help.
God wants to help us, but he wants us to ask him.

Even though we mostly use prayers to ask for help, there are many different forms of prayers.

Here are some examples of different forms of prayers:

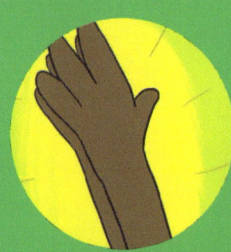

PRAYER OF AGREEMENT (corporate prayer Acts 2:42)

Example: This is simply praying in groups, as small as two or three, or as big as the world.

PRAYER OF FAITH (James 5:15)
Example: Having the body of believers praying for a person or persons.

PRAYER OF PETITION OR REQUEST (Philippians 4:6)
Example: Is asking God for help.

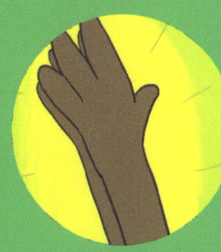

PRAYER OF THANKSGIVING (Psalm 95:2-3)
Example: This is simply giving thanks to God for all his gifts and blessings.

PRAYER OF WORSHIP (Mathew 6:10)
Example: Using prayer to give glory and praise.

PRAYER OF CONSECRATION AND DEDICATION (Mathew 26:39).

Example: To pray for God to make you holy or clean, or to dedicate to a higher calling.

PRAYER OF INTERCESSION (1Timothy 2:1)

Example:

This is praying to God on the behalf of someone else.

PRAYER OF IMPRESSION

Example: This is praying for someone because you had a feeling, not based on evidence.

PRAYING IN THE SPIRIT (Ephesians 6:18)

Example: This is praying in a heavenly language that may not be understood by others.

Anytime is a good time to pray. When we pray, God wants us to pray in the Spirit.

The posture of our hearts is more important than how we position our bodies. God wants our hearts to be humble, honest, and in faith believing that he hears us. However, my favorite time to pray is just before bedtime.

When is your favorite time to pray?
I mostly pray three times a day. I thank God in the mornings when I wake-up. I pray the prayer of thanksgiving, over my meals, during the day. I also pray just before bedtime. Even though this is my routine, sometimes it changes because things happen, but I still use the opportunity to pray.

When I am at church, and my pastor asks
if anyone has a prayer request, sometimes I raise my hands.
Prayer request gives everyone at church the opportunity
to pray for that person in a group setting.
This type of prayer is called Intercession.
My great grandmother is sick, and we intercede for her to get well.

Do you know of anyone who needs prayer? Maybe you know of someone who is in trouble, hurt, sick, homeless, or hungry.
We can use prayer to pray for so many things.

If everyone prays for someone, we are helping each other.

This is how Jesus teaches us to pray:
"'Our Father in heaven,
hallowed be your name,
your kingdom come,
your will be done,
on earth as it is in heaven.
Give us today our daily bread.
And forgive us our debts,
as we also have forgiven our debtors.
And lead us not into temptation,
but deliver us from the evil one.

PRAYER OF PETITION

My mom has Asthma, and I use this prayer of Petition to pray for her healing.

God, I pray that Asthma will leave my mother's body forever.

God, please help my mom; heal her completely, in Jesus' name.

If you or someone you know is in trouble, and they need help.

Quickly call on Jesus, and he will help!

PRAYER OF INTERCESSIONS

Lord, we pray for the world, that it will change for the better.

We intercede for the people on earth that they will have your peace.

We pray that sickness will leave people's bodies,

and the homeless will find shelter

In Jesus' name amen

PRAYER OF THANKSGIVING IN THE MORNING

God, I thank you for everything you have done.
Thank you for waking me up today.
I thank you for providing rest,
food, love, and care.
God, you provide everything
I need, and I am thankful.

PRAYER OF THANKSGIVING AND BLESSING FOR FOOD

God, I thank you for providing food for us.
Please bless this food for our bodies
and provide food for those that are hungry.
We praise and thank you, in Jesus name, I pray amen.

PRAYER OF PROTECTION

God, I pray that you will protect me when I am asleep.
I pray that my sleep will be well.
I pray that no weapons formed against me shall prosper,
and I will be safe in Jesus' name, amen.

ABOUT THE ILLUSTRATOR

Dehstin is thirteen, the oldest of three children. As an older brother, the role of helper is very familiar and rewarding at times. His mom Nadine Miller-Campbell saw his talent as a Story-Time Animator and asked him to help her illustrate this book, Daniel's Book of Prayers. Dehstin enjoys playing the guitar, listening to music, drawing, and animating. Dehstin uses his animating skills to make videos on his YouTube channel, Alphamations1.

Some other works that he has done:

Illustrated Blissfulness 22 Avatar and Channel Banner.

Assistant Graphics Editor of Dehstinie's Dreams

Illustrate and write comics for Living Water Home Educators Class

Featured at the Sterling High School Art Fair in 2016

He enjoyed illustrating every page in this book and hopes that you will enjoy his work. alphamations1@gmail.com.

ABOUT THE AUTHORS

DANIEL CAMPBELL

Daniel Campbell is a fun-loving, seven years old boy, who loves to share and care for others around him. He is exceptional at serving, and enjoys reading, playing games, and praying. He has a healthy curiosity for the things of God.

Daniel is a New Jersey native, with strong Jamaican influences. He has the privilege of being homeschooled and truly enjoys the benefits. He hopes to be a pastor, marries a lovely wife, and have three beautiful children when he is older. Daniel's parents believe strongly in preparing their children for the future. He is encouraged to dream about his future education, career, family, and spirituality. Daniel believes that he can start to prepare for his future by praying about his dreams and aspirations.

NADINE MILLER-CAMPBELL

Nadine is an outgoing, joyful, and loving person. She enjoys homeschooling her three children, traveling, and public speaking. She is talented with words and uses the platform of an author to bring her words to life. She remembered her mother and father telling her stories as a child. Hence, she became fascinated with folktales and literature. Her husband, Conrad is her biggest supporter; they are the founders of Connecting Hearts with Arts Ministry, Inkspired 365, The Party Professionals LL C, and To Have & to Hold Ministry. She has also published these books:

- A Self-Expression of My Emotions
- The Mission
- What Kind of Love Are You Producing?
- Dehstinie's Dreams

Don't forget to give your review on Amazon.com or google.com

I am looking forward to hearing from you.

Let's Stay Connected
- If you are inspired
- If you want to join our prayer group
- If you have been impacted by this book
- If you want to learn more about this prayer movement

Please follow us on:

 inkspired_author

 www.prayerworkscafe.com

 authorfanspage

 inkspired365@gmail.com

 Inkspired 365

 prayerworkscafe@gmail.com

www.ingramcontent.com/pod-product-compliance
Lightning Source LLC
Chambersburg PA
CBHW042127040426
42450CB00002B/105